MORE THAN ENOUGH

LOVE

http://www.love2liveway.com

Picture taken by Oscar Benson

BY

Oz

Oscar Benson

A living human being on planet Earth

Oscar Benson   More Than Enough

DEDICATION

I would like to dedicate this book to all the martyrs. Many
have died trying to change the world to become a better
place to live and love and enjoy our gifts that have been
given us.

Introduction

"The greatest of these is LOVE"

There always has been more than enough of everything on earth.

We have just had limited access to and understanding of it all. Today more than ever before in the short history of man on planet earth it is becoming astoundingly known that this statement is true.

We only live on less than three percent of all the land on earth. Some have made the case that we could actually all fit inside the borders of the state of Texas in the USA. We use less than three percent of the current values and resources that have been placed here for us to find and use. The whole of the land and its environment is capable of supporting more people than is presently on earth by at least 100 times over. [Multiply 7.5 billion by 100.] In other words there is enough of every kind of food, wealth, place, joy, excitement, housing, creativity, love, happiness, comfort, peace, and any other amenity that humans would like or want in their lives to live, even time.

Problem is however that we are using some resources, like trees, that would best be less used and other resources, industrial hemp or zero point energy/free energy, we are not using much at all. We have been living unwisely and under duress of artificial scarcity.

Many reading these statements immediately may find fault with me and quote what you have been told or read in your books of the past. This is because you believe that which you have been told or more specifically not told, and you fail to have understood the reality, which in fact is that there is and has always been more than enough of everything you need but not the money in the system to buy it with. The problem has been that those in power have always kept/limited us from having or attaining what we needed to truly live in freedom here on earth. They operated in power, hate and control. They deal out scarcity and aggravation not fulfillment of Love.

Let me give you my definition of love:

Love is the action of beneficence of one to others even to the point mental/physical exhaustion or even the physical death of the giver. This beneficence can and often lasts from generation to generation as well as it can minister to a single individual in a single moment of time.

Love does indeed conquer all evil. When you allow people to have time to think and you appreciate what comes from each and every one of them, then they will tell you of the positive creativities inside of them that have been placed there as gifts. These gifts and talents unlock the secrets of the storehouses of value that are in the world.

Nothing has ever truly been lacking in our journey here on this planet. It was either never discovered or uncovered. Every plant, every person, every animal or fish, has a purpose for living here on this planet.

When you have the positive world view and understanding then nothing is impossible or lacking for your every need to be met and with great abundance.

Many of the things here are still hidden from most of the people. But the internet and the ability to visit with one another is helping the people of the world to begin to realize that they have been indeed limited by those people who are not walking in love and respecting the planet and its limitless value, nor are they loving and respecting the people of the planet and their wondrous value.

We have proved to be valuable to one another in so many and various ways. But history {his story} has tried to hide from us our separate values and understandings and has there by limited the ways that we would have associated with one another and helped one another to develop those gifts that have been found here on this great planet.

For instance, there has always been a searching for the fountain of youth. This has been done by ruthless and selfish individuals for their own malignant purposes of lording themselves over others. There have always seemed to be these stupid individuals who try to work against love and against sharing of the values that have been given humanity on this great planet.

They have sought after the secrets to immortality when in fact immortality is a given they just reject because it doesn't suit their stupid idea of how it should be given. All over the world there has been a constant seeking for that which has no real value. Instead of respecting our immortality of spirit and learning to love the gifts and the giver they have maligned their original purpose and sought after that which is of little value to all.

When we seek after those things that are truly valuable to all and share them, then all will prosper and all will have more than enough and peace and joy of existence will reign instead of kings, monopolies, and tyrannical governments as we see on the world today.

The Occupy movement helped to send the message to the one percent that the ninety-nine percent are waking up. In the days to come you may see their panic as they realize that their days of selfish rule are nearing an end. Their houses of cards are falling in on them because of their lack of love and appreciation of humanity and their lack of confidence in the gifts of humanity and their love for the planet that has given all people opportunities for sustainability of life.

IN Short their greed for power is bringing them down. Power corrupts and absolute power corrupts absolutely. The ones that have been doing their bidding in the past are no longer willing to or they are usurping the authorities above them for their own piece of the pie.

When we seek to actually love all around us and understand all around us then we support the good in all and build a society of respect, responsibility and tolerance including joy and love that benefits us all and the planet and it's varied other inhabitants. This kind of respect and acceptance of responsibility has always been what heroes are made of. But because there have been those who deny you the information of the other peoples then it has been difficult to appreciate or follow those heroes and their gifts.

1

Energy

There is and always has been an abundance of energy for the people of the world to use and this energy is such that it will not pollute the world or harm the world. This energy has been known about since around 1900. For more than 100 years there has been this type of energy that has been kept from us and our knowledge of it has been severely limited.

Had we learned about it from the very beginning then many things would be available in our lives. Cars would today be riding above the ground so no need to make roads or tear up the grass. We could have all the necessary energies to explore other new and exciting worlds in fact. Through these explorations would come the greater knowledge and if we love the things we find there and don't just exploit them, we may find that inner space travel would be common place today and not just a movie setting.

These energies had they been given freely to the masses would have made it so that the people of the world would not be starving. Instead though people are not living in peace and joy and when you subject them to torturous lives then they will indeed multiply themselves and there will be a multitude of negative emotions and energies as the world has seen under the regimes of the past 4000 years. When the people live in peace and love then they utilize their times more effectively to sustain the good living and don't try to destroy through fear.

An ancient Native American man named Chief Dan George [1]once said, "What people don't understand they fear. What they fear they try to destroy."

The man who brought this understanding to my world is a brother of mine. He told me of a man named Nikola Tesla[2], who after stroking a cat and finding static electricity began to research the phenomena and came to the solution that in a small amount of space is infinite energy stored. This energy is today called zero point energy. All over the world people are tapping into this energy and developing many new valuable machines to extract and develop this energy. In the process of doing this they also have uncovered antigravity and particle beam technology[3] and square wave healing technology.

---

[1] .If you talk to the animals they will talk with you and you will know each other. If you do not talk to them you will not know them and what you do not know, you will fear. What one fears, one destroys.

http://www.searchquotes.com/quotation/If_you_talk_to_the_animals_they_will_talk_with_you_and_you_will_know_each_other._If_you_do_not_talk_/417387/ .

[2] Nikola Tesla the forgotten genius; http://www.viewzone.com/tesla.html

The man that the entire world knows because of propaganda is Thomas Edison[4]. However, Thomas Edison was not as smart as Nikola Tesla but instead was just more deviant and evil and controlling. He would pay little boys to bring him dogs and cats and then on a stage in front of the people he would electrocute these animals and claim that Nikola Tesla's AC (alternating current) was to blame and that it was dangerous to use and thereby tried his best to malign him to the people of America. T. Edison even electrocuted an Elephant named Topsy on Coney Island in New York City in 1903. Later Publishers for books of high schools and colleges of higher learning would do similarly and often left Nikola Tesla completely out of nearly every book.   Until the days of the internet there was not much known of this mighty, brilliant and considerate human being Nikola Tesla. J. P. Morgan, when he found that Nikola Tesla

---

[3] Particle beams; http://www.reformation.org/tesla-and-tunguska.html

[4] Propaganda of Thomas Alva Edison;
http://jawadonweb.com/?page_id=900

wanted to bring free light to the entire world and knew he could do it, J. P. Morgan then jerked his monetary support away from Nikola Tesla and this caused Nikola Tesla terrible problems. Nikola Tesla was indeed an extraordinary and accomplished scientist and not a business man. Some say that Thomas Edison was a better scientist due to the fact of having more patents to his name. He basically stole the majority of the ideas from others. When Nikola Tesla warned him about the dangers of X-Ray, he, being arrogant and a fool, ignored Nikola Tesla's advice and put some of his own workers to testing X-Ray. Edison finally dropped X-ray research around 1903 after the death of Clarence Madison Dally who died horribly from it after having both his arms amputated. T. Edison was not much more than an exploitative evil person trying to steal from those around him. None of his workers were allowed to patent their ideas while working for him.

When Nikola Tesla went to work on one of his inventions for him, Tesla was promised $50,000[5] if he could make it work. He made it work and went for payment and was told by Edison that it was just a joke, concerning the $50,000 and then ordered him to be paid simple low wages for his time and Nikola Tesla walked away from him. Then later Nikola Tesla proved him wrong to the world. Had Edison had his way with the D.C.(direct current) grid for all of us to buy energy for lights it would have cost a huge amount more and exploited the earth in far worse ways because of the much greater need for copper for wiring and other resources for creating the electricity to reach across the world. AC uses less copper and carries more power than DC does and you need fewer power plants to produce AC than you need for DC.

Nikola Tesla was able to bring light from the Earth with no wires connecting a switch and a light together. When he would turn on the switch, the light a great distance away would light up. He proved that it was possible to bring light and electrical power to people in a

[5] War of currents AC DC   http://www.youtube.com/watch?v=iEJNJ0rFSe8

simple and non-pollutive, nonintrusive way[6].   Nikola Tesla was one of the original inventors of Free Energy and Zero Point Energy.

Governments, monopolies and the military establishment as far back as the 1940's have known of much of this energy and power and they have used it but kept it from the masses. They have limited our access again to that which by rights had been given of the creator of the world and should belong to all the people of the world. This stupidity to deny us our rights was foolish on their part. This has created in us a hatred of them and when the time comes and the people begin to realize what we have been denied, there will come a reckoning and those individuals who are still to be found trying to live in that paradigm will be hunted and they will be begging the very rocks of the world to fall upon

---

[6] Nonintrusive vs. Smart Meter

http://powerelectronics.com/alternative-energy/who-needs-smart-meters-when-theres-non-intrusive-load-monitoring

them and cover them from those of the world that they have repressed for so very long.

The leaders of the governments and today the monopolies of the world have committed mass murder and severe atrocities against the humanity of the world and against the world itself and against the creator of the world they have had no respect and denied his/her very existence. It is not we the people of the world who have sought with our energies to destroy the world. We for the most part have operated in ignorance, which was thrust upon us by our leaders and those in large corporations and institutions that hid the truths from us. They secretly, purposefully denied the existence of the values of this world and sought to use our energies of value in wrong ways by pitting the peoples of the world against one another through hatred and bigotry and racial discriminations in order that we may destroy ourselves completely. These covert operations are coming to light now and the peoples are beginning to understand and see openly that which they have tried to cover and hide all these many years!!

Free energy is a thing of the present and future. We all around the world will soon be utilizing it in so many creative ways that will astound and amaze us daily. With it we will solve the problems of the ever encroaching deserts of this planet and deliver healthy foods to all of humanity and deliver ourselves from the bondage of the pollution filled debt slavery of the past.

With it will also come new ways of travel and freedom of travel with no more of the restrictions that have kept us from knowing and experiencing all of the creators gifts that make this planet we live on worthy of our respect and love and appreciation. With this new found knowledge we will solve the problems of the industrial revolution and the pillage that it has wreaked upon the world that sustains our very lives and there will be healing of the pollution that these stupid controllers have forced upon humanity and our environment. People, animals and plants alike will thrive and flourish in the future.

There is a large amount of information concerning this abundance of energy and many people today are finding out more and more daily about it in experiments in every continent on earth. The oil companies/monopolies have killed many brilliant inventors and threatened death to others in the past hundred years trying to keep this knowledge from coming into our hands. People like ......Joseph Newman, Stanley Meyer, Charles Pogue, John Bedini[7], Frank Fecera, Mikhail Dmitriev, Shen He Wang[8], Perendev, D. Le May, Howard Johnson, Harold Ewing, Nikola Tesla, Mehran Tavakoli Keshe[9] and so very many others to name here now, [10] have often given their lives to

---

[7] Bidini school girl motor ;
http://www.eternaltruth.net/Science/Bedini%20and%20the%20School%20Girl%20Motor.htm

[8] Wang Shen He;
http://peswiki.com/index.php/Directory:Wang_Shum_Ho_Generator

[9] Free Energy, Plasma generators that provide healing energy, and energy that can clean up the environment.   www.keshefoundation.org

study and find new ways of doing things. They have invented the likes of magnetic motors, hydrogen generators, free energy devices, and many other novel, exciting and useful machines and processes. Many of these inventions have been lost[11] to us as well due to the persecution of the inventors by monopolistic corporations and their greed for power and control. Necessity is the mother of invention. There has always been a dire need for humanity to find a way to free abundant clean renewable stable energy.

Having free abundant energy is the key to not only our quality of life but likely it will even prove to be of vast importance to our survival as a planet in the solar system. If the powers that were (banks, governments, monopolies)

---

[10] Patrick Kelly's book , "A Practical Guide to 'Free Energy' Devices, http://www.free-energy-info.co.uk/PJKBook.html You can download a 2500 page book here with all the information and up to date information needed to make your own devices to run your own cars and power your own houses and businesses here.

[11] Lost inventions of Nikola Tesla; http://altered-states.net/barry/tesla/index.htm

continue to exploit the earth the way they have throughout the past hundred years and continue to exploit the human energies like they have through millennia then we are all doomed to extinction like many of the animals and plants in recent times. Contrary to popular belief it is not the individual that is polluting the earth but the 'individual-less' corporations in the name of profit who are polluting and destroying the green and blue world that is sustaining our present lives.

Lastly, in no way will the advent of free energy destroy the markets of the world. Instead it will enrich the markets by releasing the creative forces so long held captive by the fiat money printers of the world.

Oscar Benson   More Than Enough

2

Wealth

There has always been more than enough wealth in the world for every person to share and I mean every single person. Currently today there are estimated to be around seven and a half billion people on our lovely planet. Many think that there are too many people and therefore not enough wealth to go around.

"The top elite's goal is to create world government and scarcity memes are incredibly helpful to this process. By artificially suppressing the amount of oil available in the world, the power elite continues to manipulate society and move it toward its long-awaited <u>New World Order</u>.

But as a result of the Internet, the ability of the elites to support its scarcity-based propaganda is failing. We are seeing more and more evidences of this lack of control. The utter implosion of the Kony 2012 video campaign is but one example. <u>Global warming</u>, the "war against terror" and "<u>vaccines</u> are a cure-all" all are memes in various stages of collapse."

The above is a quote from The Daily Bell.[12]

If you add up all the gold and all the diamonds and all the other wealth/value of the world then you divide this number by the number of people you would come to a figure of about five billion dollars. That is right. Each and every one of the people could have about $5,000,000,000[13] [14]dollars to do with as they like.

---

[12] .http://www.thedailybell.com/3716/The-Big-Lie-of-Peak-Oil-Now-Confirmed   .

[13] Heaather Anne Tucci-Jarraf

It is a known fact that the family of Nicky Oppenheimer has been for years storing all the diamonds to keep an artificial price so high that most of the people of the world cannot afford to buy any. Recently he has sold his 40% of De Beers to a mining company in England called Anglo-American. Believe me Anglo-American will most likely continue with hoarding them for the same reason. Diamonds are a common stone. The price should be according to its true value and not the inflated value of denying others from having it and forcing our minds to think of it as only a luxury. The same can be said of many of the materials that are in the world. Our understanding of economics as has been taught to us through history is faulty. We are taught of the price in relation to supply and demand and not in relation to our own energetic value or that of the worlds.

---

http://www.scribd.com/doc/118067922/PARADIGM-DOCUMENT-FROM-THE-TREASURY-FINANCE-AG-INDUSTRIESTRASSE-21-CH-6055ALPNACH-DORF-SWITZERLAND

[14] Heather Anne Tucci-Jarraf http://oppt-in.com/cvac/

This knowledge is indeed where supply of truth is limited. So people make a decision to limit the supply and artificially drive up the price. The banks today even do this with money. This is how they forced us into debt slavery.

A new video[15] just came to my knowledge and it talks about a resource based economy. If all the resources of the world are indeed equally available to all then there would be no need for money is the contention of Mr. Jacque Fresco.[16] He is much more articulate than I am on the subjects of what to do to save the world. From all I have seen he has some great ideas. All of us probably can come up with some great ideas if we simply would not have to spend/waste our time making those fools in government and monopolistic businesses rich all the time.

---

[15] . http://thevenusproject.com/en/download/paradise-or-oblivion
Video by Jacque Fresco

[16] . http://thevenusproject.com/the-venus-project/resource-based-economy

I agree with him that there are more than enough resources for us all on planet earth and we only need understand how to develop them in such a way as to benefit earth and then ourselves.

When the wealth of the world is considered not something to horde but rather something to share then the whole of the world reaps the benefit and not just the one percent who then try to regulate/manipulate the rest.

Banks should not be private institutions[17]. Never should there be interest attached to loans. Compound interest should be outlawed throughout the world.

---

[17]Carrol Quigley - the bankers' plan

"The Power of financial capitalism had [a] far reaching plan, nothing less than to create a world system of financial control in private hands able to dominate the political system of each country and the economy of the world as a whole.
This system was to be controlled in a feudalistic fashion by the central banks of the world acting in concert, by secret agreements arrived at in frequent meetings and conferences.
The apex of the system was to be the Bank for International Settlements in Basel, Switzerland, a private bank owned and controlled by the world's

central banks, which were themselves private corporations.
Each central bank sought to dominate its government by its ability to control
treasury loans, to manipulate foreign exchanges, to influence the level of
economic activity in the country, and to influence co-operative politicians by
subsequent rewards in the business world."
Carrol Quigley, Tragedy and Hope, 1966 - [Bill Clinton's mentor and
Georgetown University professor]

Mark Evans - Global Financial Institutions

The "big five" prime banks of Wall Street, the owners of the "Class A" stock
of the NewYork Federal Reserve Bank, are: Chase-Manhattan, Citibank,
Guaranty Trust, Chemical/Manufacturers-Hannover, and Bankers' Trust. The
Class A stock of the Federal Reserve has not been sold or traded on the open
market since it was hermetically sealed from the public at the end of the
summer of 1914. It is the exclusive property of Wall Street and European
prime banks, whose major stockholders are the trans-Atlantic Ruling Class.
This pattern holds true of Central Banks throughout the nations of the
advanced capitalist sector. The Big Five have interlocking directorates with
the "Seven Sisters," the Anglo-Dutch-American oil cartels: Exxon, BP
(British Petroleum), Dutch-Royal Shell, Texaco, Mobil, Gulf, and Standard
Oil of California (SOCAL).

Several of these trans-Atlantic money and commodity cartels financed
Mussolini and Hitler and actively maintained their connections with the
Reich throughout World War II. They were also all actively involved in
Stalin's Russia by the beginning of the first Five Year Plan in 1928. None of
this is really secret-anyone can discover the facts by doing a little research.
Nor should it be considered a "conspiracy" (either by those who promote or
deny the essential facts of the matter) - bankers and businessmen have been
"trading with the enemy" for centuries. It is just one more example of "the
wise investment policy" of cartels like J.P. Morgan and Co. and Standard Oil
of New Jersey.

the capabilities of humanity that create an actual increase in overall wealth.

When people are indeed free financially and have abundance of energy they will create a new and better world-wide environment peacefully. It is the stress of never having enough to meet individual needs that causes many to not want to live in a beneficial manner to their fellows.

Politicians amenable to the objectives of financial capitalism, and academies prolific with ideas for world control useful to the international bankers, are kept in line with a system of rewards and penalties. In the early 1930s the guiding vehicle for this international system of financial and political control, called by Quigley the "apex of the system," was the Bank for International Settlements in Basle, Switzerland. The B.I.S. apex continued its work during World War II as the medium through which the bankers — who apparently were not at war with each other — continued a mutually beneficial exchange of ideas, information, and planning for the post-war world. As one writer has observed, war made no difference to the international bankers:

.http://www.bilderberg.org/bis.htm .

We for 100 years in America now have been living under a 'private-money-for-public-use' system. When countries like the former Muammar Gaddafi[18] [19] lead Libya were living under a 'public-money-for-private-use' system, they were prospering abundantly. In Libya prior to the 2012 illegal war against it by the U. N. (United Nations, a puppet of the privately owned Bank of International Settlements), the people were living in great freedom and prosperity. The majority of the people of Libya loved Gaddafi[20]. They paid the actual value, which is about $.14 ~ $.17 cents a gallon for fuel not an inflated value like the rest of the world which is between $2.50 to more than $5.00 dollars per gallon.

---

[18] Muamar Gaddafi   www.youtube.com/watch?v=2Jeon6PJ8HQ

[19] http://www.thetotalcollapse.com/who-is-muammar-gaddafi-lies-vs-truth/

[20] http://gmiah.hubpages.com/hub/Was-Muammar-Gaddafi-Really-A-Bad-Person

Not to mention the Libyans also did not spend any money on electricity for their houses and when married were given some $50,000 dollars to buy their first house. The Libyans[21] also had their own national bank which issued interest free loans to the Libyan government and were trying to get all of Africa to follow their lead to make the world a better place by only accepting real currency or gold for oil which really pissed the BIS, IMF and FED Reserve banks off and thus they were invaded and destroyed. Iran also doesn't charge interest on loans and in America it is illegal to loan money without charging interest. Lately the French have invaded Mali[22] and are after the gold[23]reserves there. Go figure.

---

[21] http://www.atimes.com/atimes/Middle_East/MD14Ak02.html and the lists go on and on.

[22] French invasion of Mali
http://presstv.com/detail/2013/01/14/283503/france-invasion-of-mali-preplanned/

[23] Gold reserves and uranium http://rehmat1.com/2013/01/15/french-imperialism-from-libya-to-mali/

Shell Oil is just one of the oil monopolies which make an average of £ 2,000,000[24] English Pounds per hour (+$ 3,000,000 USD)[25]. These inflated prices rob us all of our individual energies personally to pay for this outrageous act of theft. This is why the oil companies have fought tooth and nail to keep you limited as to your understanding of what other energy resources there are and how to use them personally. You are being taken advantage of severely and have been for many years.

---

[24] Shell Oil profits per hour;
http://www.guardian.co.uk/business/2012/feb/02/shell-profits-up-54-percent-oil

[25] currency conversion

http://www.xe.com/currencyconverter/convert/?Amount=2000000&From=GBP&To=USD&image.x=48&image.y=10&image=Submit

They have lead us to thinking that we are running out of oil (Peak oil, [26]supply and demand[27]) and we have been accepting what they say to us about it so that we would not seek any other than what they allow you to use or know. But those days are over.

---

[26] http://rense.com/general85/peak.htm.

[27] The hoax of Peak Oil-namely the argument that the oil production has hit the point where more than half all reserves have been used and the world is on the downslope of oil at cheap price and abundant quantity-has enabled this costly fraud to continue since the invasion of Iraq in 2003 with the help of key banks, oil traders and big oil majors. Washington is trying to shift blame, as always, to Arab OPEC producers. The problem is not a lack of crude oil supply. In fact the world is in over-supply now. Yet the price climbs relentlessly higher. Why? The answer lies in what are clearly deliberate US government policies that permit the unbridled oil price manipulations.

World Oil Demand Flat, Prices Boom

The chief market strategist for one of the world's leading oil industry banks, David Kelly, of J.P. Morgan Funds, recently admitted something telling to the Washington Post, "One of the things I think is very important to realize is that the growth in the world oil consumption is not that strong." http://themech.proboards.com/index.cgi?board=nature&action=display&thread=998

We will not believe what the oil monopolies tell us any longer and we will take back our planet and hold it gently in the future and not allow it to be so exploited as before.

When the wealth of the world is considered not something to horde but rather something to share then the whole of the world reaps the benefit and not just the one percent who then try to regulate/manipulate the rest.

Oscar Benson   More Than Enough

3

Health

The Quality of Life is directly proportionate to our quality of health. You cannot have an appreciable existence without a healthy body and a healthy mind.

Here again the people of the world have been horribly denied what the planet and our given earth will supply for us freely.

Indeed all that needs be done to maintain the majority of our health is in the wealth of knowledge that is not included in our text books and taught in our schools. For thousands of years there have been understandings and usages of plants and other substances like silver and water on our planet to maintain a high standard of health in many of the separate clans that have existed. Much of the knowledge of the past is in what is called Chinese Traditional Medicine.[28]   While it is true that modern medicine has done many wonders such as open heart surgery the majority of the ways to maintain true healthy conditions in our lives should be focused on first protecting ourselves from contaminants and toxins and then upon providing ourselves with real nutrition not the watered down fakes and lies that have been forced upon us by the FDA and their partners in crime the large drug companies/monopolies and the institutions of the medical community such as the Cancer Society or other proponents of pseudo science.

These liars including the meat and food industrial giants are all only for profit and killers of humanity. They currently control whole societies around the world and it all started just over a hundred years ago for most of us with a man called Louis Pasteur. He said that all bacteria are unhealthy, or at least that is what people think today because of all that has been said and done in his name. The pasteurization of milk and fruit juices and other products leads to the annihilation of good bacteria and enzymes that help us to have healthy bodies and live longer higher quality lives. People like Dr. Edward Howell did significant research into what true nutrition is for our bodies and wrote about it in books like "Enzyme Nutrition"[29]. He discovered that enzymes are extremely valuable to our life and longevity here on this beautiful planet.

---

[28] Iatrology, www.iatrology-boods.com/Chinese-Medicine/

[29] The Weston A. Price Foundation, www.westonaprice.org/nutrition-greats/edward-howell

He supported also the studies of earlier individuals like Pierre Jacques Antoine Bechamp (1816 - 1908) [30]who wrote that diseases of the body were caused by poor nutrition and toxins that created acidity in our bodies and thus created cellular destruction which then led to the whole host of malady and disease. The medical community however stood to gain huge profits (they don't care about health) by promulgating the trash that came from Louis Pasteur and therefore never published widely the important research that Mr. Antoine Bechamp had given to the health and prosperity of the world's people. Thus we the people had been limited again and suffering and damage and death was caused and forced upon humanity by a very few stupid, selfish people.

Love is the only smart way to live and love shares the good and eschews that which does not benefit others.

---

[30] Natural News.com,

Proof of what is told by knowledgeable and smart people like Bechamp and others are in the modern works of groups like the Gerson Institute.[31]   Dr. Max Gerson wrote a book called "A Cancer Therapy: Results of 50 Cases[32]   There is a lot of misinformation in the world today. Bad people who want to make more and more money[33] on cancer[34] will certainly lie to you and deceive you in any way they can to support their selfish ways.

---

www.naturalnews.com/030384_Louis_pasteur_disease.html

[31] Gerson Institute,   www.gerson.org   3844 Adams Ave. San Diego, Ca. +1 619-685-5353

[32] http://www.cancure.org/legislation_already_passed.htm ..New laws are being passed in some states to allow alternative treatments which will in fact offer you cures and not just prolonged existence under post cancer/radiation treatment.

[33] Written by Rick Cantrell

The below is absolutely 100% true and, as a doctor, I have been telling people this for 15 years now. No one wants to listen. Folks need to wake up. Cancer treatment is about making money. It is a 120 billion dollar a year industry in the United States alone, and estimated to be a 600 billion dollar a year industry worldwide. ..

[34] NCI's budget for FY 2010 was $5.1* billion, excluding the additional $1.3* billion in American Recovery and Reinvestment Act funds received by

A successful cancer case, according to the American Cancer Society and the American College of Oncology and Hematology, means that the person survives for 5 years. Both the American Cancer Society and the American College of Oncology and Hematology admit that a person is likely to survive cancer for 7 to 10 years even if they do absolutely NOTHING. Of course, only the doctors get those magazines - not you, the cancer patient.

This lack of love and lack of respect for fellow humans is largely responsible for the rise of the now quickly falling house of cards which is the Bank of International Settlements and the Federal Reserve System. People are

---

the Institute for spending in FY 2009 and FY 2010. Overall, NCI's budget has been relatively flat in recent years. During the period from 2005 through 2010, the NCI budget averaged $4.9* billion per year.

http://www.cancer.gov/cancertopics/factsheet/NCI/research-funding

The National Cancer Institute funded by congress of the US> have known of cures and therapies and preventions but have neglected to let us know because they make so much money from it all!!

beginning to wake up to who the liars are and why they are lying to the entire world.

There are also the testimonies of centenarians. People that have lived more than 100 years are called centenarians. One man in particular named Li Ching-Yuen[35], seems to be held in controversy for the moment and he died in 1933. Some say he was born in 1667, He himself claimed to be born in 1736. Not only did Mr. Li eat a nutritional diet of herbs and other natural foods but he also understood that the thinking of a man was extremely important as well. The words of Mr. Li Ching-Yuen are these:

"Keep a quiet heart, sit like a tortoise, walk sprightly like a pigeon and sleep like a dog."

As I said, health of the body as well as the mind is what is needed for true quality of life. We live in a toxic environment today and it is toxic not only physiologically, but psychologically as well.

We are under constant duress of information overload and false and mostly absent needed truths in publications not to mention debilitating emotional distractions from every side. We have the TV which in my opinion is one of the major culprits that destroy peace of mind mostly by distracting us from talking to one another and by not delivering to us the whole truth about any given thing that is or could be important to us. It is so funny how people will sit in front of the box (like in Orson Well's "1984") and agree with everything they see. Then there is radio which constantly repeats the same songs 'of the top ten' so that we can only think of those lines or melodies no matter where we go. There are sounds that lend to healing in your body and mind but you won't find them in the 'top ten' because they are not making any corporations lots of money. Humans need more than what is being put on our plate. Love depends upon trust.

---

35 www.theepochtimes.com/n2/health/lessons-about-longevity-from-a-256-year-old-152740.html

If we can't trust the bank and can't trust our governments and because of all their stressful ways can't even trust one another then no wonder there are people who hurt others and even murder others, even the innocent.

Our minds and bodies are regenerative by nature, by creation. We should be able to live much longer and have a far greater capacity to enjoy our lives than most of us do. We should not be confined to hospital beds or wheel chairs or insane asylums. We were meant to be free. We were meant to smile. We were meant to live in harmony with ourselves and others and the world.[36] Please check out the understandings that some are coming to know.

1. Jealousy can cause cancer and weaken the immune system.

2. Seeking Revenge can lead to insomnia and throat disease.

---

[36] http://humansarefree.com/2013/03/the-256-year-old-chinese-herbalist.html

3. Inability to find a solution to a situation can cause lung problems.

4. Lacking moral principals - causes chronic diseases, infections, and skin diseases.

5. Being too categorical or unwavering in beliefs - causes diabetes, migraines, and inflammations.

6. Lying causes alcoholism, fungal infections, and weakens the immune system.

7. Aggressiveness causes gastric ulcers, acid reflux, and warts.

8. Reticence causes schizophrenia and kidney diseases.

9. Cruelty causes epilepsy, asthma, and anemia.

10. Seeking conflicts causes thyroid enlargement.

11. Apathy causes diabetes.

12. Inconsistency or being fickle causes infertility.

13. Being rude or insulting causes diabetes and heart diseases.

14. Anxiety causes digestive system disorders, heart, and skin diseases.

15. Greed causes cancerous diseases, obesity, and heart diseases.

These are 15 situations listed on the website called Humans are Free.com.

The inability to find a solution to a situation is an interesting ailment than can cause serious illness. When you are constantly distracted by all the media hype and absolute BULLSHIT that is spewed out at you daily it is no wonder that you may feel confused and unable to distinguish what the next step you should take would be.

Some today are beginning to realize that the keys to our saving our planet must come from with-in us, from with-in our own minds, and not from the oligarchical rulers that we have been taught to cow down too.

There is a group called the Keshe Foundation[37] who is using a new machine that can cure many things such as gang green and diabetes which causes your body to waste or rot away. Instead of amputation they treat the body and the body heals from within.

---

[37] Free Energy and Healing Energy   http://www.keshefoundation.org
http://www.youtube.com/watch?v=QVbasNBlm7E&feature=share

This group needs our support as the powers that are trying to control the world don't want these kinds of information/technologies and help to be heard of or used by people.   Look at the Rife[38] machine. It was used in the 1930's to the 1950's to heal many people of all sorts of problems/diseases. Now it is made illegal in many states to sell or use.

Water[39] itself is a healing agent. People mostly don't drink enough water to clean their bodies at all. Much the contrary they drink all sorts of sodas and sugary fruit flavored drinks and these destroy the bodies PH balance and lend to the causes of disease.

Take a new born baby for instance. When it is born its skin is so soft and comfortable. Look then at most old people and you will see that their skin is dry and non flexible and easy to tear. This is always attributed to age.

---

[38] ..Rife square wave machine http://www.rifevideos.com

[39] The Water Cure http://www.watercure.com

You can see that the older person has a body chemistry that lacks moisture. Older people often have about 70% water in their bodies while babies are nearly 90% water content. Drink more water if you want to live a healthy life. Pure and simple it is.

As the list above shows, our attitudes are creative forces. When we have an attitude that draws us into helping others and sharing with others then what happens is that our health and well being increases and we become more powerful and satisfied in our lives and relationships. We need more power in and over our lives. Don't let others steal your energy.

Oscar Benson   More Than Enough

4

Security

The politicians and bureaucrats we have looked to in the past really do not care about our personal security. There are more than enough of us to protect ourselves by teaching one another to love. There is even more than enough time to do it as well. The problem is we spend all our time working for our debt slave masters or listening to their mind controlling screen (T.V.) and no time do we spend working on our own ideas and working with our neighbors on their ideas. These, the ideas and realities produced of our neighbors are the things that matter most.

Oscar Benson

More Than Enough

We spend too much time in Walmart and too much time buying the latest toy or watching the latest T. V. show. We should be using our time building our security for ourselves. We should use our time by investing it in our own personal increases in knowledge and love.

We will never have a good environment or lovingly comfortable place on planet earth if we continue with the same paradigm we have been living under these last one hundred and more years. Change is a must. We must make different decisions if we want a different future.

In the world today there are so many security issues. Most of them are simply ridiculous. With the 911[40] incident the American people and many around the world became subject to increased prison-like security, privacy invasion and difficulty in travel.

---

[40]   TSA'S Grip on Internal Travel is Tightening.

Why Louis Freeh Should Be Investigated For 9/11

http://www.911truth.org.

I firmly believe and will stake my reputation as an educated individual on the fact that the whole thing was a false flag event designed to goad the American populations support of the US governments/ international bankers desires to attack Iraq. There were no weapons of mass destruction even though this was a constant saying in the news. There was however an Iraqi idea to not continue to allow payment for oil only in American dollars issued by the Federal Reserve Bank which is a part of the international banking cartel. Iraq had already been beaten before and the only reason that we were put into this predicament was because Hussein wanted to change the way he was paid for his country's oil. Here again the Bank of International Settlements and the men who own it and the Federal Reserve banks wanted and still want all in the world to use only their fiat currency so that they can continue their control over the peoples of the world. If the people are allowed to live debt free then others will begin to know what it is like to be free and then they will have lost all they have worked for in all these last 500 years or so.

There is an old saying; behold the ants and their work. When you take the time to watch the ants then you will be amazed at what they do and how they mindlessly support one another and work with one another. They have their own jobs to do and yet they don't mind helping another because they all have a single purpose as well as an individual purpose to live out. Our singular/individual purpose can and will be completed and more easily if we too help others to complete the overall purpose of our existence here on this wonder filled planet. That purpose is to experience the Creator's creation and to help others do the same.

The evil ones (formerly due to UCC filings by Peoples Trust 1776) in power don't mind giving hints as to what they were doing but they don't want to let the cats out of the bag entirely.

We have been in a constant terrorist war [41]for the past 12+ years.   This war on terror and the war on drugs are both just a cover for the banksters to take control over more and more of the worlds peoples and put them into debt slavery and to destroy the abilities of the countries to maintain their original public banking facilities or sovereignty.   They have all been converted into U.N. controlled slave states. The U. S. backs and supports and fights where ever the U. N. says to go. The U.N. is patently controlled by the World Banks private owners, Rothschild, Rockefeller and Morgan families.

---

[41] The terrorist war officially began with Bush 2. But in reality it was begun many years earlier before even the war between Russia and Afghanistan http://www.bibliotecapleyades.net/sociopolitica/sociopol_waronterror57.htm .

Oscar Benson   More Than Enough

5

Earth

"She groans unto that day"

There is more than enough land on Earth for all of us and many more. The Queen of England is said to own 16% of the best lands of the world. Well if all the people of the world only live on less than 3% then she could easily give up some of the best lands for the sake of the poor couldn't she? There is more than enough!!! There has always been more than enough. 500 years ago the British, the French, the Dutch, the Portuguese and the Spanish were instrumental in terrorizing and raping the indigenous peoples of the world and robbing them of their natural resources and they are continuing today to do the same to basically all the peoples of the world. What do you think AUSTERITY and Carbon (CO_2[42]) tax

---

[42] An interview with 'the father of global warming'. The paper was published in 1975 and the warming trend began again in 1976, but this was sheer luck. It turned out that the periodic cooling shown in the ice cores was not borne out by ice cores in other places, even within Greenland.

So, for two different prizes that I won, I was introduced as "the father of

plans are?   They are clamping down harder and harder on the people of the world in the name of imperialism and slavery. The governments of the world who are putting these austerity measures in place are cowling down to the banksters and their henchmen. John Perkins wrote a book called the "Confessions of an Economic Hit Man".[43] To understand more about the issues you may also go to this movie called "The End of Poverty". [44] This is an historical account of how the world came to know poverty and why. There is more than enough of everything on earth and we need only begin to understand that if we are to live a good life here then we must stand up together and take control of our lives by doing and being responsibly and lovingly.

---

global warming" because of this one lucky paper I wrote that was partially wrong, instead of being known for sixty years of science.

http://membercentral.aaas.org/blogs/scientia/interview-father-global-warming

We are seeing huge changes today and tomorrow we will see even more. This won't happen overnight but it will come to pass.

The land is rich with life for all of humanity. We must become squatters if you will and begin to walk onto the lands belonging to the large corporations and if they are using the land in ways that are detrimental to life on earth then we must stop them. We nor the earth can afford this evil any longer. Look at how many GMO crops are threatening the existence of the bees and the original safe and healthy crops of the world. The Mexican [45]indigenou s people are fighting GMO's desperately that are being put on the land by Monsanto and we should help them.

The oceans belong to the world and to the people of the world and not the monopolies or corporations or governments. The people should have the freedom to travel them or fish in them or sail on them but not the ones who destroy them and pillage them.

[43] www.economichitman.com and you can go to www.johnperkins.com

[44] We need to know about why poverty exists;

http://youtu.be/pktOXJr1vOQ;

The governments support the monopoly oil companies drilling and polluting[46] them but I don't. I think the majority of the people in the world agree with me. The same with the rivers and streams and lakes; we, the people own them and don't want the drug companies dumping their chemical soup into them and destroying the delicately balanced life therein.

In the past the monopolies have continued to make the rules and regulations stiffer against individuals and more and more relaxed against the corporations. Some laws say that corporate entities can only be fined so much per day for any violations. When the same oil companies make 5 million dollars an hour a fine of say $250,000 or even 5 million dollars a day is nothing to them.

---

[45] .Monsanto Co. seeks to take over Mexico's heartland with GM maize http://digitaljournal.com/article/337459#ixzz2Osn5kbSb

[46] .BP has caused so much damage to the environment that may take even centuries to over come. HOW much more can we or the world take of their total disregard for us and the world?

Besides a fine only is reflected in their bottom line/profit and this can easily be adjusted by raising the price a portion of a percentage and the cost then is directed against the people who purchase the products from the monopoly and not the company itself what so ever!!![47] When the public cries out for accountability it only gets those poor escape goats tossed to the wind (sometimes murdered) but never the corporate hierarchy.

The five big oil companies posted 137 billion in profits for 2011.[48] BP made 3 million dollars an hour during 2011 and this was done in spite of the fact that they were responsible for the very biggest oil spill in the history of the world.

---

http://www.globalresearch.ca/did-bp-cause-damage-to-the-gulf-sea-floor-ever-larger-natural-oil-seeps-from-the-giant-macondo-reservoir/29685

[47] BP doesn't fuel America it fools America.
http://www.bbc.co.uk/news/business-20336898

[48] The five big oil monopolies that control the governments of the world.
http://wakeup-world.com/2012/02/18/bp-made-3-million-per-hour-in-2011-

They (the banks, oil, insurance, drug, war machine builders, all monopolies) all lobby congress to have laws written in favor of their needs constantly and pay out millions to different congressmen and senators for multiple millions of subsidies as well as changes in laws that directly affect them and prosper their businesses. The whole system is tragically devastating to the world and to the people and animals, birds and sea creatures and will never stop as long as we allow them to be above the law as they are today.

The trees are being cut for no good reason today. They are being cut because of industrial giants who don't care about the world and some of the groups that purport to protect the trees are themselves infiltrated with spies and agents of the monopolies.   But there are ways that we can go around them.   Start planting Marijuana for replacement of trees in industry. Marijuana can be used for so many purposes that it is amazing and it actually

while-spill-victims-continued-to-suffer/

helps clean the environment and restore the balance of nature.   The drug wars[49] stopped the industrial production of hemp in America and now it has begun again in Canada and there is a lot of wealth in the production of hemp that is being denied the people of America and other countries.

SAVE THE TREES!!! SAVE THE PEOPLE!!!

We must begin to look at other ways to grow and produce products to meet our needs rather than to destroy our planet and its means of helping us to survive. Recently there has been a huge undertaking by the people who are commonly called heads in my times past. Today you can find that Marijuana[50] is a plant that has a multitude of uses.

---

[49]Multilateral Control & Syndicate Crime (1907-1940).Led by Protestant clergy and laity, a global anti-opium movement created mass support for the imposition of legal controls over individual drug abuse, culminating in a

However, almost all of the good beneficial uses of Cannabis are currently illegal in most countries of the world due solely to the "Drug Wars"[51] which were promulgated and fought by several of the supposedly legal (DEA,FBI, CIA[52], Army, Border Patrol, Judicial systems, Coast Guard, US Marshals, and Drug Task Force Agents) entities of the corporate United States of America. By the US making these wars on terrorist and drugs a part of all the recent treaties of commerce between nations (see footnote 38 above), they have enacted war against the many peoples of the world without a formal declaration and under force of keeping radiation and policy that regulate more safely and easily eradicated by simple educational means.

series of treaties that restricted the global narcotics trade.
Starting with the Shanghai Opium Commission of 1909 and the International Opium Conference at The Hague in 1911-1912, these early meetings led to a succession of opium control treaties under the League of Nations in 1925 and the United Nations after 1945.

On balance, the most profound and lasting legacy of this movement remains the ideology for conceptualizing and applying radical law and policy that regulate what individuals do to and with their own bodies. The intrusion of the state into a realm previously thought personal and private marks a small but still significant watershed in modern political history.

Over the space of two centuries, China had thus progressed from opium importer to heroin exporter through the intersection of three key factors--a global commodity trade in opiates, the failure of successive interdiction campaigns, and an alliance between drug syndicates and military intelligence services.

http://www.opioids.com/opium/history/index.html.

[50] . Marijuana, Cannabis Sativa, Hemp
http://www.informationdistillery.com/hemp.htm

Many hundreds of thousands of people, if not millions, have been killed needlessly all over the world due to these two illegal and illegitimate acts of state and the benefits monetarily gained by those individuals in the various governments and monopolies involved. First the several countries supported wars in order to sell the opiates and then they began to fight wars to prevent the opiates from being sold all over the world. What an absolute mess!! All of it can be laid to the destructive forces of monopolies and government involvement in helping to establish them and their subsequent protection of them.[53]

---

[51] Drug War Objective?
http://en.wikipedia.org/wiki/Opium_Production_in_Afghanistan.

[52] The Politics of Heroin:
CIA Complicity in the Global Drug Trade..

http://www.barnesandnoble.com/w/the-politics-of-heroin-alfred-w-mccoy/1111886256

[53] Moreover, an informal alliance among four intelligence services--Thai, American, French and Nationalist Chinese--played a catalytic role in promoting the production of opium in northern Laos and the Shan Plateau of

This all can and should be reversed. Just look at the recent numbers of countries such as Portugal[54], that are decriminalizing[55] the use and sale of drugs and the numbers of people that are steadily decreasing their use because of that. Changes are long overdue. If we will get together and support good changes then we will see the world become a much brighter and safer and healthier place to live in. Love and wisdom will work wonders if it is not limited as before. Freedom of choice is helping people to become free from addictions. It is a truth that if

northern Burma. In particular, the Nationalist Chinese (Kuomintang, or KMT) occupation in 1950, combined with the Shan secessionist revolt after 1958, transformed the Shan States into a region of conflict that reduced government control and allowed a marked expansion in local opium production.
http://www.opioids.com/opium/history/index.html.

[54] .Decriminalization of drugs is long overdue.
http://www.time.com/time/health/article/0,8599,1893946,00.html

[55] There are still opponents to Portugal but the people there and other countries are seeing good results and moving to do the same around the world. http://www.spiegel.de/international/europe/evaluating-drug-decriminalization-in-portugal-12-years-later-a-891060.html.

you tell someone they cannot do something then they will do it just out of spite!! Vice should not be regulated or criminalized whatsoever.

There is more than enough knowledge in our world to help all the people to live better than the last 4000 years and especially the last 100 years!!

The vice laws that criminalized the use and production of alcohol during the prohibition days in America only made the rich richer and killed the small producers or jailed them and forever caused problems in our society. There are more than 2,000,000 people in prison today in the land of the 'FREE[56]. This is a travesty of justice if ever there was one. These people are mostly held against their will because of some vice or another and not for actually having done some harm to others.

---

[56] The prison industry supplies the world's cheapest labor for the monopolies and is the most horrendous and heinous of crimes yet perpetrated against the people of the Americas.

Some are imprisoned because of creating minted pieces of silver[57] they were using that was competition to the privately owned banks. Some are held for selling natural herbs. Some were incarcerated for preaching against homosexuality(now considered a hate crime), just selling organic raw milk (which people have been living off of since the beginning of time) or saying something against an authority figure.[58] [59] [60]

.http://www.globalresearch.ca/the-prison-industry-in-the-united-states-big-business-or-a-new-form-of-slavery/8289 .

[57] .. http://en.wikipedia.org/wiki/Liberty_Dollar Notice that on the face of the wiki it states that the article is bias..

http://www.dailypaul.com/279953/gata-still-not-sentenced-bernad-von-nothaus-liberty-dollar-moves-for-acquittal-or-retrial.

[58] .http://saharareporters.com/news-page/nigerias-secret-police-summons-pastor-bakare-over-fiery-sunday-sermon-asking-president-jon.

[59] ..http://www.usmarshalsmuseum.com/sedition_acts .These people were arrested and later released but since the Patriot act was established as law there have been many arrested and still incarcerated.

[60] In part the National Defense Authorization Act helps to preserve the status quo established a decade ago with the original provisions in the PATRIOT Act giving the government broad new powers in the so-called War on

Our Constitution and Bill of Rights were supposed to guarantee the freedom of being able to say whatever we like about or to whomever we want so long as it is true!!

Let people do as they like with their own bodies and lives and speech. Let them have the rights of privacy and the world will go along a lot smoother and happier. When you deny peoples their basic rights to privacy and their ownership and use of what is theirs then you will find yourself in a fight that is not necessary nor wanted nor productive!!

John Pilger [61] concludes: "We need not accept any of this if we recognize that there are now two superpowers.

Terror. In part the bill expands those powers, codifying the use of indefinite detention of foreign nationals and possibly US citizens arrested abroad and at home..

.http://www.forbes.com/sites/erikkain/2012/01/02/president-obama-signed-the-national-defense-authorization-act-now-what/.

[61] http://johnpilger.com/videos/breaking-the-silence-truth-and-lies-in-the-war-on-terror   John Pilger

One is the regime in Washington the other is public opinion now stirring all over the world. Make no mistake it is an epic struggle. The alternative is not just conquest of far away countries; it is the conquest of us, of our minds, our humanity and our self-respect. If we remain silent, victory over us is assured."

'Breaking the Silence: Truth And Lies In The War On Terror' was a Carlton Television production for ITV first broadcast on ITV1, 22 September 2003. Directors: John Pilger and Steve Connelly. Producer: Chris Martin.

Awards: The Chris Statuette in the War & Peace division, Chris Awards, Columbus International Film & Video Festival, Ohio, 2004...

Oscar Benson   More Than Enough

6

Solutions

There has already been set up a possible solution to all the woes that face our existence here on this lovely orb, in the tiny solar system, which is part of; what is way more than enough of the great infinity of space and creation.

Most people look at the world's problems from a paradigm similar to watching a hurricane or tornado. They see all these objects (problems) flying around and hear the roar (media) loudly in their ears and sense the eminent fear (reactions of others) all about them and don't know which proverbial fire to put out first. The actions and situations that appear to them are not the actual cause that spins before them. Instead the cause is a simple high and low coming too close together. The problems [62](all of them) on our little orb are all laying at the feet of the Bank[63] owners[64] of the world. There are only a small

---

[62] ..As Napoleon pointed out: "Terrorism, War & Bankruptcy are caused by the privatization of money, issued as a debt and compounded by interest "- he cancelled debt and interest in France - hence the Battle of Waterloo. ... http://rense.com/general79/tril.htm   Rockefeller and Rothschild

[63] MAYER AMSCHEL'S WILL

"Let me issue and control a Nation's money and I care not who makes its laws".

Biographer Frederic Morton, in The Rothschilds, tells us that Mayer Amschel Rothschild and his five sons were *"wizards"* of finance, and *"fiendish calculators"* who were motivated by a *"demonic drive"* to succeed in their secret undertakings.
http://www.biblebelievers.org.au/slavery.htm .

number of them and they have been in absolute control of every government that has bought into their private-money-for-public-use system for more time than most of us have been living on planet earth. They have kept us in a position of scarcity for far too long.

All of the media which the bankers[65] own allow only the printing of what will not harm or uncover their

---

[64] .http://www.thebirdman.org/Index/Others/Others-Doc-Jews/+Doc-Jews-National&InternationalConspiracy&NWO/AmericanCivilWarCausedByJews-WillieMartin.htm

..The good Czar, after several unsuccessful attempts on his life, was murdered in 1881. Lincoln was murdered in 1865, on April 4th, by an actor, John Wilkes Booth, in whose trunk was found coded messages the key to which was found in Judah P. Benjamin's possession. Benjamin escaped to England where he later died. The Czar, Alexander II, had been responsible on September 19, 1861, by imperial decree, for emancipating the Russian serfs, in number over 47-million. Serfdom in Russia was ended by the stroke of a pen. But in the United States, it took billions of dollars and oceans of blood to free three million, not serfs, but slaves, because of an infamous plot of English and European Jewish money lords.

.

[65] . http://en.wikipedia.org/wiki/N_M_Rothschild_%26_Sons

motives and plans and guilt. They own politicians by virtue of every evil way you may imagine from just plain offerings of bribery to extortion and murder such as was the case of John F. Kennedy[66]. You can find these truths in the statements made by them over the years. The average citizen has had no time to research these situations and mostly rely upon the screaming of the media about the hurricanes that blow wildly through our lives such as 911(a definite false flag event). We are so easily influenced that we are even have become very predictable.

"Give me the control of the credit of a nation, and I care not who makes the laws."

The famous boastful statement of Nathaniel Meyer Rothschild, speaking to a group of international bankers, 1912

---

[66] . http://nstarzone.com/JFK.html   "For example, he (JFK) had plans to abolish the Federal Reserve System, which prints worthless money backed by nothing, and charges interest on it, making us a debtor nation to a group of international bankers."

Hopefully that will change soon and we will with the help of the internet and open-mindedness begin to refute the lies and the fears that come at us daily and begin to teach those around us how stand against the bankers who have sought to enslave us and destroy us through their various subterfuges..[67]

This solution we so desperately need, calls for changing every corporate monopoly and corporate government into a trust. The trust would be similar to the one called "One Peoples Trust 1776".[68] The idea is novel in many respects.

---

[67] "Give me the control of the credit of a nation, and I care not who makes the laws." The famous boastful statement of Nathaniel Meyer Rothschild, speaking to a group of international bankers, 1912: "The few who could understand the system (cheque, money, credits) will either be so interested in its profits, or so dependent on its favours, that there will be no opposition from that class, while on the other hand, the great body of people, mentally incapable of comprehending the tremendous advantage that capital derives from the system, will bear its burdens without complaint, and perhaps without even suspecting that the system is inimical to their interests." The boastful statement by Rothschild Bros. of London. ..
http://rense.com/general79/tril.htm

[68] This   http://www.peoplestrust1776.org

It would change all of these monopolistic companies/corporations, governments and institutions to nonprofit organizations. These organizations would then have all the profits reverted to the people of the world. This would be similar to the old cooperatives that sought to be competitive in the late nineteenth and early twentieth century's.

This is not far from the Resource based economy that I mentioned earlier which is proposed by Jacque Fresco.

Another organization that is publishing solutions is called "Thrive". Thrive is the group that was begun by Foster Gamble and his wife. Mr. Gamble has traveled the world and come to the conclusion that is similar to Heather Anne Tucci-Jarraf also has come to. Another of the people that has made some considerable changes for the people in Ecuador is President[69].[70]   President Rafael

---

[69] President Correa and how others view him..
http://www.plaidavenger.com/leaders/profile/rafael-correa/

[70] President Correa plot to assassinate by U.S.
http://axisoflogic.com/artman/publish/Article_65294.shtml

Correa is loved[71] by his people and hated by the rich and the rulers of the rest of the world at large for his righteous stands against the political injustices of the world and the illegal banking practices that have kept the majority of the worlds population in debt slavery for so long.

When the products like GM gas cars or large monopolistic electrical services of the presently failing monopolistic organizations become unwanted then they should either be no longer produced or other products that are wanted should replace them. A huge blunder was when the U.S. corporate government bailed out the banks and AIG and GM and other large monolithic companies that have been doing bad business and needed instead to be closed. What should have happened is that money should have been spread out to the people of the nation and the US would have had a huge increase in jobs and opportunities that would have forestalled and reestablished it as a leader in the world financially and creatively.

---

[71] Why the Ecuadorians love Correa..

http://www.guardian.co.uk/commentisfree/2013/feb/15/rafael-correa-

This was the bankers and government's foolishness that brought down their house of cards.

Today in the world there are many new ways to produce electricity that make it possible to have better transportation choices that are far less polluting and much more responsive than the inner combustion engines have been in the past. These however are mostly used by the individuals around the world who have made them for themselves. For the future all of the inner combustion engines can either be converted to hydrogen usage (or other new technologies that produce zero amounts of pollutants) or yanked out and electric motors installed at a minimum charge. Think about the jobs this would create and how much cleaner our lives would be. These electric motors can then be run on a battery pack that has a completely enclosed charging system using Zero-point energy/Free energy devices. So the needs for further exploitation of the earth's mineral resources are not even necessary to fill the need for the battery systems. The

---

ecuador-elections .

systems won't even be needed because of the types of zero point energy systems that will be created.

This would change the world in a very short time and cut the pollution greatly as well as cut the need for so much oil production.

These type of energy motors and similar ones like the Wang colloidal magnetic motor are currently being installed in major applications in countries like China to replace the usage of coal in the coal fired electric power plants. When all the coal and nuclear power plants are changed over to Zero point energy devices this too will relieve the stress of the people of the world and they will be able to focus their increased productivities and energies to creating many better ways of living and doing and being.

When people have large amounts of free time and plenty of resources then the world will change overnight. People are very resourceful given enough time. Sure some may not work and that is and has always been true. But more would be working in America after welfare money is no longer available. If the people have enough money which could really happen if all the money in the hands of the richest 4% were equally spread around then those who don't want to work wouldn't have to. But believe me I would rather do something than die of boredom.

I think most are like me. Few would lounge away to nothing. Given they could travel or do whatever they like so long as they harm no others then life would truly take on a whole new meaning for everyone.

For one they will have a tremendous increase in time to better use in quality education and management of their house hold and families. These advantages of saved time and energy and money will create huge differences in how people associate with one another and interact in the world.

This will usher in a peace that has before never been known.

7

Peace

We truly can have more than enough peace. We must come together in ways that support one another and not deny one another our freedoms of choice and freedoms of culture. True there will never be 100% agreements for every one because we are all different. But we should stop trying to control one another as the former regimes have done to us over these last 4000 years.

When it comes to law there should be no such thing as vice law. Whether a person of any age decides to drink or smoke something or whether they decide to engage in what ever activity so long as it has no ill effect on others then they should have that unalienable right. People should develop the boldness to tell others when they wish they would smoke somewhere else or to stop doing or start doing something beneficial rather than depending on a government entity to do so for them.

When I say that so long as it doesn't harm any others I am speaking of the former laws called common laws. In common law there is no such thing as someone being harmed by another without there being some physical contact. Were you hit or bruised. Now when it comes to your energy then that is defined lately and given a value. Your individual capability to produce is considered your energy and it is covered under UCC law, because it has a monetary value. An injury to your body cannot be as easily remedied and therefore is covered under common law.

There is and can be more than enough love and peace for all of us to live and thrive on planet EARTH.

The End

Please, if you liked or thought anything of this book, leave a review on it in your honest opinion that others may know what you think of it.
Thanks,

Oz

About the Author

Oscar Benson

Oz is my pen name and has been since I was 15. My grandmother didn't like Oscar so she named me Ozzie and my Grandfather called me Oz.

I was born in Oklahoma and was the oldest son of a retired Army sergeant. I started writing poetry and later after many years of biblical study began to write essays. I have always been a passionate person. I too have always desired to see a better life on our lovely orb not only for myself but for all the people of the world.

I served two enlistments in the military. One was in the Navy during the last of the Vietnam War and the other in the National Guard prior to the 1st invasion of Iraq.

I believe that there are two schools of wisdom. One is of course the school of hard knocks. The second is by being still and listening to your creator. When you give him your undivided attention he will speak to you and help you to see truths and ways that you never knew existed.

I have traveled extensively throughout the United States (lower 48) of America and Mexico. I also have been to other countries of South America and the Middle East and the Orient. I have lived in the Philippines, Mexico, and China for several years each. I was living in the Philippines under Martial Law during the Marcos regime. I heard the people dying in the streets from midnight to six a.m.

I have seen poverty first hand. I have seen wealth first hand. There is a huge difference between the two that shouldn't be there. Our present system in the world is extremely flawed. I hope that this book and others like it will be read by many young people who will change the world and that tomorrow's world will be one of peace and love and life!

I have seen and walked the Amazon and the mountains of China and America. I have seen the wildernesses, deserts and rainforests of the world. I know that there are many many lands that are habitable and yet lay untouched. I have seen the largest cities and watched the squirming masses. I know that there is without a doubt more than enough.

Bibliography

Alfred W. McCoy (1 May 2003)

The Politics of Heroin: CIA Complicity in the Global Drug Trade..

Georgetown University professor]

John Perkins (2 Feb 2006) Confessions of an Economic Hit Man: The shocking story of how America really took over the world

F. William Engdahl* The Reason For Soaring Oil Prices - Pt II 5-22-2008 http://themech.proboards.com/index.cgi?board=nature&action=display&thread=998

Frederic Morton, Biographer 21 Aug 1991

The Rothschilds: A Family Portrait

http://www.biblebelievers.org.au/slavery.htm .

Carrol Quigley Tragedy and Hope, 1966 - [Bill Clinton's mentor and

When he died on September 19, 1812, the founder of the House of

Rothschild left a will that was just days old. In it, he laid down specific laws by which the House that bore his name would operate in future year.

The laws were as follows:

(1) All key positions in the House of Rothschild were to be held by members of the family, and not by hired hands. Only male members of the family were allowed to participate in the business.

The eldest son of the eldest son was to be the head of the family unless the majority of the rest of the family agreed otherwise. It was for this exceptional reason that Nathan, who was particularly brilliant, was appointed head of the House of Rothschild in 1812.

(2) The family was to intermarry with their own first and second cousins, thus preserving the vast fortune. This rule was strictly adhered to early on but later, when other rich Jewish banking houses came on the scene, it was relaxed to allow some of the Rothschilds to marry selected members of the new elite.

(3) Amschel forbade his heirs "most explicitly, in any circumstances whatever, to have any public inventory made by the courts, or otherwise, of my estate .... Also I forbid any legal action and any publication of the value of the inheritance .... Anyone

who disregards these provisions and takes any kind of action which conflicts with them will immediately be regarded as having disputed the will, and shall suffer the consequences of so doing."

(4) Rothschild ordered a perpetual family partnership and provided that the female members of the family, their husbands and children should receive their interest in the estate subject to the management of the male members. They were to have no part in the management of the business. Anyone who disputed this arrangement would lose their interest in the Estate. (The last stipulation was specifically designed to seal the mouths of anyone who might feel like breaking with the family. Rothschild obviously felt that there were a lot of things under the family 'rug' that should never see the light of day).

The mighty strength of the House of Rothschild was based on a variety of important factors:

(A) Complete secrecy resulting from total family control of all business dealings;

(B) An uncanny, one could almost say a supernatural ability to see what lay ahead and to take full advantage of it. The whole family was driven by an insatiable lust for the accumulation of wealth and power, and

(C)   Total ruthlessness in all business dealings.

Rick Cantrell

Cancer treatment is about making money...provoking thoughts.

http://algarvedailynews.com/features/health-a-beauty/4924-cancer-treatment-is-about-making-moneyprovoking-thoughts

Fereydoon   Batmanghelidj (Jun 2003)

Your Body's Many Cries for Water: A   Revolutionary Natural   Way   to   Prevent Illness   and   Restore   Good Healthhttp://www.amazon.co.uk/Your-Bodys-Many-Cries-Water/dp/1903571499

Reed Simpson and Ellen Hodgson Brown (16 Dec 2011)

Web of Debt: The Shocking Truth About Our Money System and How We Can Break Free

Nikola Tesla (15 Jun 2011)

My Inventions: The
Autobiography of Nikola
Tesla

Des Griffin (1 Jun 1980)

Descent Into Slavery

Jacque Fresco Feature Film.
Paradise or Oblivion.

http://thevenusproject.com/en/
download/paradise-or-oblivion

Oscar Benson   More Than Enough

www.ingramcontent.com/pod-product-compliance
Lightning Source LLC
Chambersburg PA
CBHW070538290526
45790CB00002B/557